HOW TO WRITE YOU BOOK

Book 2 – Writing on the Super Highway

From an Idea...

"the Editor"
Ms. Edi Tor

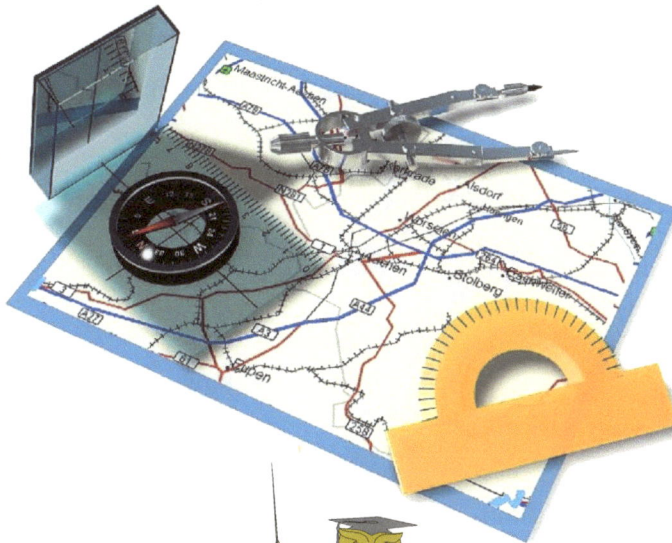

"the Publisher"
Mr. I. M. Publisher

"the Writer"
Ms. Iwanna B. Writer

to your Finished Story

as narrated by
The Three Wise Guides

Bobbi Madry & Francine Barish-Stern

Published By Golden Quill Press

a division of Barish-Stern Ltd.

P.O. Box 83

Troutville, VA 24175

Copyright ©2015

Bobbi Madry & Francine Barish-Stern

ISBN 978-0-9847330-2-6

Cover by Art on Gold, Troutville VA.

Interior Design by Kenneth A Bray, Troutville VA.

Printed by CreateSpace, An Amazon.com Company
Available from Amazon.com and other retail outlets
Available from Amazon.com and other online stores
Available from Amazon.com and other book stores
Available from Amazon.com, CreateSpace.com, and other retail outlets
A reference to an Amazon review
Available on Kindle and other devices
Available on Kindle and other retail outlets
Available on Kindle and other book stores
Available on Kindle and online stores

TABLE OF CONTENTS

GUIDE TO ROAD SIGNS

Writing Map 1   **Trip Signs:** These Writing Map Signs will identify each new chapter of your journey as a color coordinated Writing Map. Think of these signs as the Welcome Sign you see when entering a new state that you must pass through to get to your final destination. Each sign will also correspond to the downloadable Extra Bonus Travel Forms.

DO IT NOW! **Map Sign:** This sign will alert you to ATTRACTIONS worth stopping at. Visiting will help to reinforce chapter information.

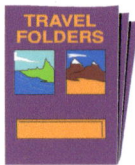

Travel Folders: Throughout this book you'll be prompted to create folders. We suggest setting up physical File Folders as well as computer files.

The Forms are divided into Example and Exercise. A Feature of The Examples is that they follow an actual book, Golden Quill Press' "Code 47 to BREV Force."

Suitcase: Finally we have to pack for the voyage— So use this SUITCASE to Pack all materials, supplies, file folders, extra forms and any other materials you will need to travel *"From an Idea...to your Finished Story."* Each chapter review will tell you what to put in your suitcase. Remember Your Suitcase is also an organizer file. It should contain everything you'll need and can be a physical file and a computer file.

Pit Stops: This book also offers interactive Service Stations placed strategically along your route to assist you in making those necessary pit stops. You will find: Web Support   — E-mail Tech Support — Forums — and   Benefits all designed to help you get back on the road. Look for these Road Signs when you need that pit stop—

 We also suggest that whenever you want to remember some point we've made or in order to trigger something specific you want to remember when you begin writing, you create a **Map Pin**. Your map pin is basically the Map Number, Page Number and Topic. Using **Map Pins will help you easily** locate that information, and get you moving on your voyage.

Travel Forms: At the end of each Chapter you will find additional forms called Travel Kit Forms- You may also be prompted to use them along your journey by

 We strongly recommend you use them at every opportunity to further your writing experience.

Writing is hard work— you began that work in Book 1 so now let's get on the Super Highway and Write, Write, Write!.

BON VOYAGE !!!

"the Writer"
Ms. Iwanna B. Writer

WHO , WHO was eating my porridge?

A Hungry Giant??

"the Editor"
Ms. Edi Tor

No, Goldilocks!

"the Publisher"
Mr. I. M. Publisher

🖉 **Writing Map 3**

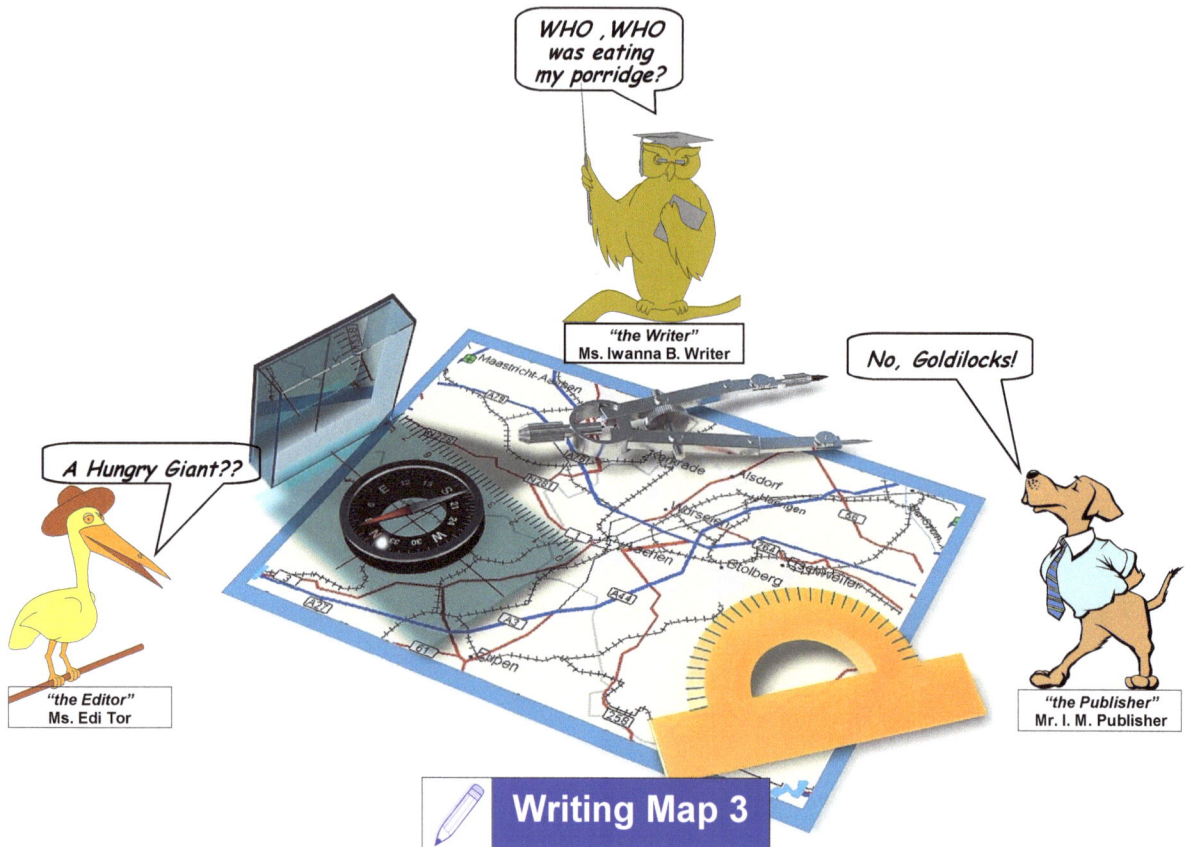

FLESHING OUT YOUR STORY

Just as an architect has a blueprint; a pilot, a flight plan and a cook, a recipe, you need to organize all the major points of your story before you begin to write. These techniques will also help you stay on track throughout your story.

Bringing Your Characters to Life

Your characters are passengers on this journey.

When you read a story in a newspaper, magazine or book, it generally centers on people. Usually it isn't about a house, but the people who live there. So, your story must create characters who come to life for your readers. Characters need to make an impression or your story will fall flat. Think of some of the simple adventure stories for children, from "Beauty and the Beast" to "The Three Little Pigs, or Goldilocks." It's easy to remember these characters because even in their simplicity, they are vibrant and almost jump off the page with life. In our creative writing workshops, beginning writers often ask, "Just how can I breathe life into my characters?" A good place to begin is to choose your main character, who is called the protagonist: the principal character of a story. This character can be the good guy, someone who champions a cause, but keep in mind, the protagonist doesn't have to be the hero.

1

On the other hand the antagonist, often the bad guy, opposes the protagonist, (main character). He or she might be an open enemy, rival, or the character that creates obstacles to be overcome. Your job is to make your characters believable and unforgettable.

Open your Travel Folder: Map #2 From Idea To Outline Form
Look at **Who**. That should be your main character—the one the majority of the story will revolve around.

My Main Character Is_____

Now let's FLESH that character out!

Go sit in the park, on a bus, stand in an aisle in the grocery store or anyplace where you can observe total strangers. Now find someone who looks right for your main character. Imagine that person playing your character in your story — Is he or she a good fit ? If not, try again until you find your perfect main character. Observing people is the best method for character development.

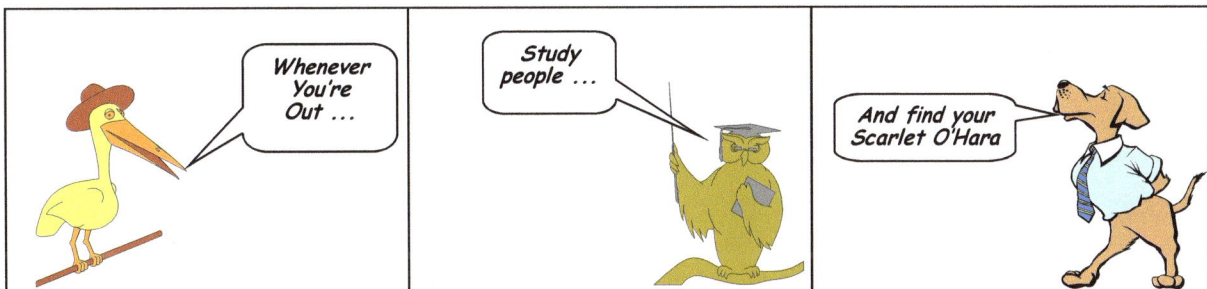

Once you've gotten a good picture of what your character should look like, you can give that character and appropriate name. **Our Experts Suggest:** The Name Game

Naming your Characters

All names have meaning and a writer has thousands of names to choose from when building characters

You can also visit your local library or book store to find a name book. An internet search for boys names or girls names will also return numerous sites of interest.

Names used in historical novels, such as Heathcliff, Esmeralda or other dated writings require more research. Names that are popular today may not have been around in the past. However, some names, especially from biblical times, never seem to go out of date. It's up to the author to choose appropriate names while keeping the reader in mind. Names that are totally wrong for the character only detract from the writer's credibility.

NAMES TELL A LOT ABOUT YOUR CHARACTERS.

Last Names can have as much impact as First Names. They tell a great deal about the character's origin's: Scarlet O'Hara, Obi Wan Kenobi. When you add a last name it can bring your character a whole new dimension: When naming characters, try to choose names that fit without obvious stereotyping. Don't give a serious character a silly name.

RHETT, SCARLETT, MICKEY MOUSE or Buster Brown Shoes?...

DO IT NOW! Choose a memorable name for your main character

Character Identity Crisis

When you begin to examine people, you'll find that real people aren't perfect. You want your characters to hold a fascination for the reader, whether they're a good character or a bad one. If they're perfect they may not be believable or interesting. Now try to study people you know. What are their personality traits? What habits do they have? What qualities distinguish them? Find their good and bad sides-- Now think of your main character and imagine that character's good traits and bad.

Without Faults and Imperfections your characters will look like Naked Skeletons

In our workshops, participants have told us it's often difficult to remember everything about their characters, especially when they have more than one or two interacting in a story. Remember you're your character's creator and in order to write believable characters you need to have a clear picture of all of your character's details. Detailing is a way for you to not only get a very clear picture of your characters, but also a way to keep all the information about those characters straight.

DO IT NOW! Get your Writing Map 3 **CHARACTER DETAILING** Form from your Travel Kit at the back of this chapter.
Decide on one Main Character Fill in all information - Repeat for others

TRAVEL FOLDERS

We suggest you take a great deal of time and really "flesh" out this part of your skeleton. The more you do now the easier it will be when you begin to write. Refer to your Travel Kit Forms often to remind you to use the   character's physical, mental and emotional makeup and to help you keep your facts about them straight.

Additional Tips

In our workshops, we learned that some writers have expressed a need for even more visual representation of their characters. We suggest you take paper, pencil and crayons and draw figures of each of your characters and then fill in the details. You don't have to be an artist—stick figures will do. Be sure to approximate size and height and fill in the color of his or her hair, eyes and other details. Some writers also build a file of interesting looking people they find in photos or in magazines to help them achieve a more visual concept of someone they want their characters to resemble.

Sometimes minor characters are written in to help move the story along. If you barely mention someone in a scene, then you should write only the necessary details. For instance, if your lead character, a Detective Sam Sharp, stops at a hot dog stand and says: "Hi Joe. How's business. Gimme one with mustard and a coke." Unless Joe has a part in the story, that can be all the reader needs to know. But suppose Joe is an undercover police officer and the hot dog stand has been set up as a front. Now we have a reason for Detective Sam to stop by the hot dog stand and we need more information about Joe..

It's important to have a reason for people, places or things in a scene, but superfluous details bog down your story and bore the reader. Props can be used effectively to help flesh out your character, but they must have a purpose. If Detective Sam stands by the hot dog stand, he must have a reason. He may sip coffee, or tie his shoe—all the while exchanging information with Joe, but to anyone who might be watching, the scene would appear to be no more than two men discussing a hot dog.

Send your Character to the Casting Director

Before you begin writing, you should be sure you've created characters who will be memorable. Think of your favorite movie—and then imagine the main character as someone very different – usually it doesn't work. Now think of a character from your favorite book. Can you close your eyes and picture not only what that character looks like, but the way the character acts and speaks. Sometimes even the most insignificant character leaves a lasting impression, so don't skimp on detailing all your important characters.

The best way to check if you have created viable characters is to Go back to your **Map# 3 Character Detailing Form.** Look over the details of the main character in your story and then ask yourself whether or not a casting director could take your **Character Detailing Form** and know exactly which actor or actress should play that character in the movie.

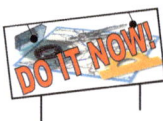

Play casting director and put your main character in the movies—

Who would play that character? _____

Why would you choose that actor/actress?

_____

_____

Now pick an insignificant character in your story and do the same--

Who would play that character? _____

Why would you choose that actor/actress?

_____

_____

Take a lesson from the producer of "Gone With The Wind," David O. Selznick. He searched and searched for the perfect actress to play Scarlet O'Hara. The character had leaped off the pages of Margaret Mitchell's book and he could see her in his mind's eye; and he didn't stop searching until he found Vivian Leigh— the perfect Scarlet. Miss Leigh made the character come to life for the movie.

So be sure your character detailing is thorough enough for you to write the next Scarlet O' Hara.

Writing Map 3

TRIP REVIEW

Map Directions

Character Skeletons Should Be Covered With Flesh

Memorable Characters Deserve Memorable Names

Let Your Words Paint A Picture Of Your Characters

Travel Instructions — Did You?

❑ Do Character Detailing for **All** your Characters
     Then add Character Detailing to your

❑ Play the Name Game

❑ Think of an Actor/Actress who could play the part
   of your Main Character

OUR GUIDES

Point You In The Right Direction

Study characters in books and movies Don't let your reader say "WHOOO was that character?"

Nobody's perfect like us – Faults make characters more believable and more interesting

Study your favorite authors. Memorable Characters create page turners.

◀ **NOTE** ▶

Whether you're interested in publishing or not, Character Detailing will save you time when writing, by helping you keep your characters information straight and accurate. Keep the information in your Travel Folder and use it whenever you refer to your characters

Writing Map 3

✏️ **Writing Map 3**	**CHARACTER DETAILING** **Travel Kit Form**

EXAMPLE: Completed Character Detailing

Name: First: Evie Middle: Rose Last: Kane

Age: 18 Date of Birth   November 8

Body type or build: Petite, Slim, fine boned

Height: 5'5" Weight: 118

Eye color: size/shape: Brown, Pear

Description: Big, Deep Set , very expressive

Hair color/Style: Auburn, Long, Wavy

Skin tone: ❑ Medium _

Facial structure: Nose: Small, straight

Lips: Full, even teeth

Face shape: Oval, high cheek bones

General Appearance: Model Like Beauty

Personal Data

Education: Norton University,
             Majoring - Science

Occupation: Student - Admin. Assist at college

Habits/Traits:

Good: Organized, energetic, caring

Bad: Vulnerable, naive

Hobbies: Designing clothing

Marital Status: Single

Children: None

Friends: Jonathan, Ginger

Likes: Boys, Beach, California

Dislikes: Lying, cheating

Ambition: Model and Design Clothing

Parents: Vivian and Martin Kane

Siblings: Brother, Twin Brad

Background (Ancestors): Grandmother Veronica Lakeland- Model and Spokesperson

Notes: Evie is just studying science to please her parents. Prefers to design her own line of clothing .

Your Main Character:

Name: First:_____ Middle: _____ Last:_____

Age: __ Date of Birth _____

Body type or build: _____

Height: _____ Weight: _____

Eye color: size/shape: _____

Description: _____

Hair color/ Style: _____

Skin tone: ❑ *Light* ❑ *Medium* ❑ *Dark* ❑ *Other*_____

Facial structure: *Nose:* _____

Lips: _____

Face shape:_____

General Appearance: _____

Personal Data

Education: _____
_____

Occupation: _____

Habits/Traits:

Good: _____

Bad: _____

Hobbies: _____

Marital Status: _____

Children: _____

Friends: _____

Likes: _____

Dislikes: _____

Ambition: _____

Parents: _____

Siblings: _____

Background (Ancestors): _____
_____

Notes: _____

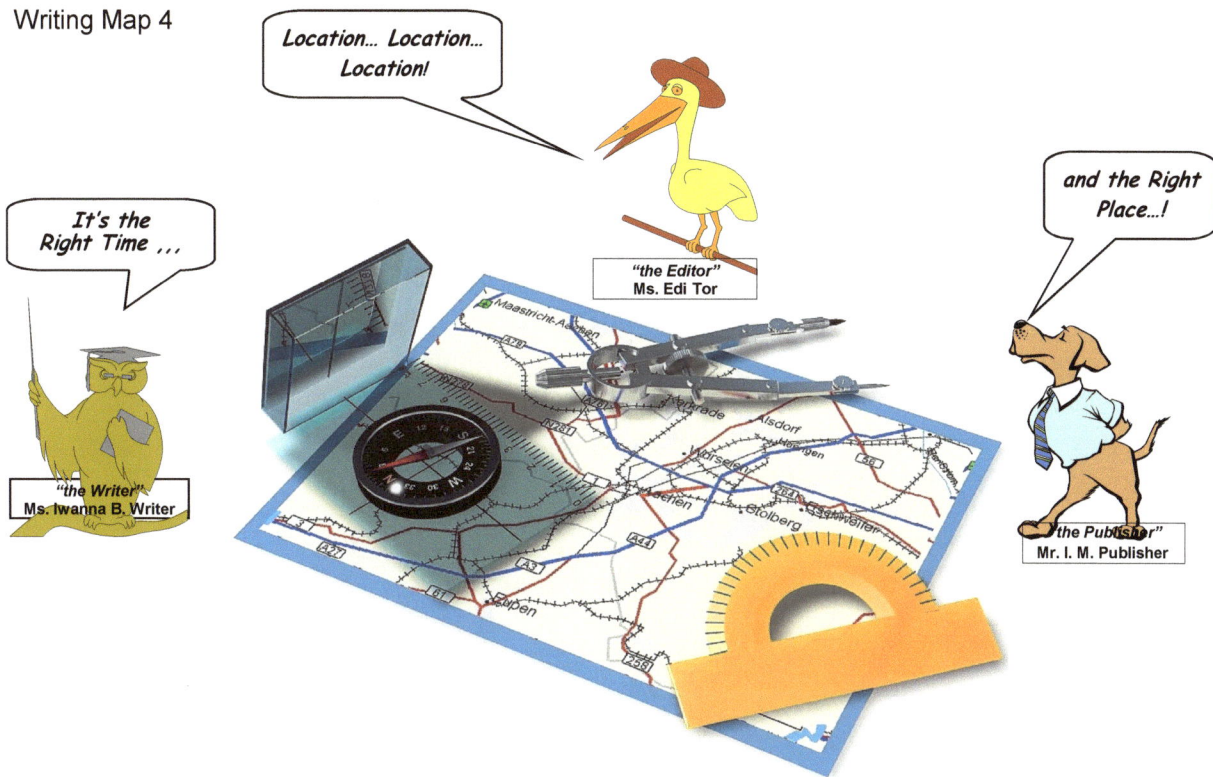

Writing Map 4

LOCATIONS, SETTINGS AND TIME

The Geographical Location —That's The Place

Once you have established your characters you'll need to put them in a geographical location: country, state, city, town or area where your story takes place. There are two types of locations: the real and the fictitious. When you describe a place that is real it's best to write about a place you know. Some writers prefer to write about exotic places, but if that is your choice, Our Writing Guides strongly suggest: do your research. Today's readers are savvy. They travel all over the world, or have seen pictures, movies, or books about far off places and now can even take an internet trip to check it out!

The best way to ensure accuracy is to visit the location you want to write about and get a sense of the sights, sounds, smells, and above all—the people. If travel is out of the question, talk to others who've been to your location. Whenever possible communicate with people who live there, get pictures, maps, descriptions and as much information as possible.

Imagined Locations

When using a fictitious place, you'll need to draw from a strong imagination. You may have an idea for a locale that is totally imagined or is influenced by a real place. Whenever possible visit that real place. When your location is totally created from your imagination, you can pull out all the stops. The more you can visualize every last detail, the more real that place will be for the reader. If your location is totally im-agined, find a quiet place and close your eyes until you can clearly envision all the de-tails of that location. Look around in your mind's eye and then use the Location   Detailing, found at he end of this Chapter, as your road map. If that location is fictitious give it a name. Whenever possible, let the name tell something about the place. For example: Peyton Place was named after the founder of the location in a book of the same name. Focus on your main location. Use as many sources as possible to get the clearest picture.

Get your Writing Map 4 **LOCATION DETAILING** Form
from your Travel Kit at the back of this chapter.
Decide on one Main Location - Repeat for additional locations
When Completed store in your Travel Folder

Next complete additional locations: (if you have more than one)

Settings

Once you've established your locations, you'll need to pick a main setting: this could be a house, an office, a park. Start to get familiar with settings by choosing a room in your character's house. Envision that room. Look around: sense the environment, the style, notice the big objects, and then turn an eye to the smallest most interesting accessories. See what this room tells you about the people who live there. If you are using settings that are unfamiliar to you, for example: Sing Sing Prison, visit the prison and the surrounding area. Be sure to talk with the town residents and with prison guards and if at all possible, even the inmates. The more you know about your setting the more realistic it will become. Again if you can't get there, do your research. There are books, movies, and other resources at your local library and book stores. The internet also provides an excellent source of information. If you put in a search for most well known places, you'll get pages and pages of information and sites to visit.

However, if you're using real places such as: "Planet Hollywood," first get written   permission to use their name. If you're using a place that doesn't have private ownership, such as The Mississippi River, you do not have to obtain permission.

9

Get your Writing Map 4 **SETTING DETAILING** Form
from your Travel Kit at the back of this chapter.
Decide on one Main Setting - Repeat for additional settings
When Completed store in your Travel Folder

Next do additional Setting: (if you have more than one)

Time

You also need to decide when in time your story will take place. If you're writing about a time period – past or present you may need to research that period to get your details right. The reader won't find your story believable if a character is wearing clothes that didn't exist or driving a car before it was invented. Even when you're writing about a time you are familiar with, and recall events, be sure that all dates and information are accurate.

Realistic Scenes

Descriptive words make other times come to life.

If your setting takes place in the 1800's, many of the things we take for granted today didn't exist. For example: think of a movie scene, where a woman is wearing a gown with a zipper, but you know zippers didn't exist until decades later. Or, how would it appear if when reading a book set in the early 1900's, the main character is using a cell phone? This error is so obvious that you'd know the cell phone doesn't belong.

When you're writing about the future you must be sure to create a time period that is different enough, but appropriate for that time. Example: If you were writing about 2010, daily travel back and forth to the moon for work may seem far fetched—but if it were 2110 it becomes much more believable. Create all the elements of that time period, and don't forget to include very vivid descriptions to help the reader grasp that time.

Get your Writing Map 4 **TIME PERIOD DETAILING** Form
from your Travel Kit at the back of this chapter.
Decide on one Main Time - Repeat for any additional Time Periods
When Completed store in your Travel Folder

Send your Locations, Settings and Time Periods to the Set and Costume Designer

Before you even begin writing your locations, settings and time periods, you should be sure you've created ones that will be memorable. Think of your favorite movie—and then imagine the story taking place in a different time period – it doesn't necessarily work. Now, think of a scene from your favorite book. Can you close your eyes and picture the way everything comes together — the place, the time and the surroundings.

10

If it's a fictitious place see how the name fits, too. That is a well written place and that is what we want you to achieve. Sometimes the most insignificant place leaves a lasting impression, so don't skimp on any details. The best way to check if you've created viable locations, setting and time periods, is to ask yourself some key questions. Could set and costume designers utilize your descriptive paragraphs and know exactly how to create your place, design the sets and obtain the accessories and costumes that are time appropriate.

Put your Main Location, Settings and Time Period in the movies—

Go back to your Writing Map 4 — Location, Setting and Time Period Detailing Forms. Look over the details and then play Set and Costume Designer.

What would the designed set location look like? _____

_____

_____

What would the main designed setting look like? _____

_____

_____

How would your character's be dressed? _____

_____

_____

What accessories need to be present to verify the correct time period? _____

_____

_____

Indian's in the middle of Manhattan in 2200—It's About Time!

But dressed in tu tus, Never!

Is that Custer ?

Our Experts Suggest

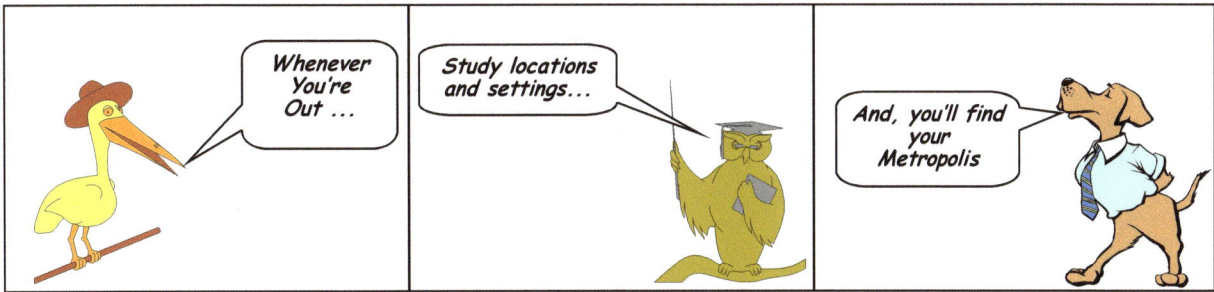

> Whenever You're Out ...

> Study locations and settings...

> And, you'll find your Metropolis

The Name Game -- Naming Your Imagined Locations

Once you're sure your Locations are Great, give them Great Names.
If your work is about New York City, then that would be the greatest name you could use,
but if you were fictionalizing New York City, what Great Name would fit that Great City —

How about > > > > > > > >

> New Washington — You know, for the Bridge?

Go back to Your — Location Detailing Form
And decide if the name of your Main Location is truly a GREAT NAME!

If you have any questions concerning any topic in Map 4 e-mail tech support
at: info@goldenquillpress.com—Subject How to Write Your Book—Map 4

Writing Map 4

TRIP REVIEW

Map Directions

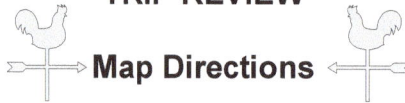

Locations, Settings & Time Periods Give More "Flesh" To The Skeleton Of Your Story
Visit Locations Or Do Your Research — Don't Play A Guessing Game
Memorable Locations, Settings & Time Periods Hold the Reader's Interest.

Travel Instructions — Did You?

❑ Do Location, Setting and Time Period Detailing

Then add Location, Setting & Time Period Detailing to your

❑ Play The Name Game for your Imagined Locations

❑ Put your Locations, Settings & Time Period in the Movies

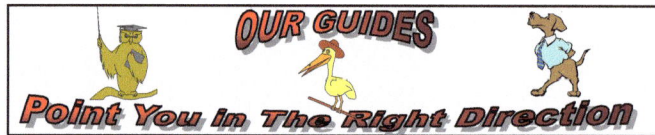

OUR GUIDES

Point You In The Right Direction

Study locations in books and movies to help you create exciting places Don't let your reader say "WHERE WAS THAT?"

We are Memorable! Places always aren't. Create Memorable Locations, Settings and Time Periods by Pecking out the details

Study your favorite authors. Memorable Places make a barking impression.

◀ **NOTE** ▶

Whether you're interested in publishing or not, the Location, Setting and Time Period Detailing forms will save you time when writing and help you keep your information straight and accurate. Keep the forms in your Travel Folders.   Use them whenever you need to refer to your Locations, Settings or Time Periods.

| ✏️ **Writing Map 4** | LOCATION DETAILING | **Travel Kit Form** |

EXAMPLE: Completed Location Detailing	**Your Main Location**

EXAMPLE: Completed Location Detailing

Name: Island Falls

Location: North Eastern United States on the Canadian Border

Type: Town in the New Hampshire

Major Industry: Education (College Town)

Population: 90,000

Average Age Range: 20-50

Average Income: 40,000 Annual

Who Lives There: Kane Family

Address: 220 Maple Street

Background: Old New England town basked in Early American history. Island Falls hosts one of the largest research facilities in the country at Norton University

Describe Location: Island Falls is college town, in the north eastern part of the United States. There are two colleges: Island Falls and Norton University. Surrounded by mountains, this town has a historic downtown core and a rural suburb, inhabited by middle and upper income residents. Compustock is the main shopping mall with brand name stores and quaint shops run by local merchants, including Vid-Mart, a new hi-tech electronics superstore. There is also a large industrial area and a new International Airport.

Your Main Location

Name: _____

Location: _____

_____

Type: _____

Major Industry: _____

Population: _____

Average Age Range: _____

Average Income: _____

Who Lives There: _____

Address: _____

Background: _____

_____

_____

_____

Describe Location:

_____

_____

_____

_____

_____

_____

_____

_____

_____

_____

_____

| ✎ **Writing Map 4** | SETTINGS DETAILING | **Travel Kit Form** |

EXAMPLE: Completed Setting Detailing

Name: The Cottage

Location: Norton University campus

Type: Secret Facility exterior and interior constructed to look like a Caretaker's House

Who Works There: Martin and Vivian Kane

Setting: A dirt road leads to an unobtrusive structure, called the Cottage, that was specifically designed to resemble a simple caretaker's house rather than the secret science research facility that it houses

Describe Setting: The Cottage, situated on a secure ten acre compound, is totally obscured from view by a thick growth of aged spruce and pine trees, and is not readily visible from the main roads around the campus. Its highly sophisticated fenceless security system prevents visitors and curious students from entering. If someone did wander onto the grounds, the security system would not allow them beyond its perimeter. Added security, cameras, motion sensors and infrared monitors are strategically positioned throughout. The Cottage basement houses the secret research facility operated by Dr. Kane.

Your Main Setting

Name: _____

Location: _____

Type: _____
_____

Who Lives/Works There: _____

Setting:
_____
_____
_____
_____
_____
_____

Describe Settings: _____
_____
_____
_____
_____
_____
_____
_____
_____
_____
_____
_____
_____
_____
_____
_____
_____
_____
_____

Writing Map 4 TIME PERIOD DETAILING Travel Kit Form

EXAMPLE: Completed Time Period Detailing

Dates: Sometime in the Near Future

Important Facts:

Oneness Cards

V-Tel

C-Tel

All Cloning is Outlawed

International Alliance of Scientists–

monitors all scientific experiments

A secret agency monitors all terrorism

threats - searches for antidotes in

case those threats become reality.

Describe Time Period: better environmental conditions, longer life spans, eradication of many diseases Scientists work independently, while having the scientific resources of a collective in order to speed up discoveries. But evil, hatred and envy are still forces to be reckoned with. Terrorism is still a major problem for the world, but most countries have vowed to work together to stop all threats. Oneness cards containing all financial and personal information are required for everyone. Technology has made many advances that make everyday life easier. Tele-portation systems are being used in big business but might soon be a way to   transport people from one place to another.

Your Time Period Detailing

Dates: _____

Important Facts:

_____

_____

_____

_____

_____

_____

_____

_____

_____

Describe Time Period:

_____

_____

_____

_____

_____

_____

_____

_____

_____

_____

_____

Let's Stop at the Plot Hotel

And, get a sub-plot

And, a good night of twists, turns and conflicts

"the Writer"
Ms. Iwanna B. Writer

"the Editor"
Ms. Edi Tor

"the Publisher"
Mr. I. M. Publisher

Writing Map 5

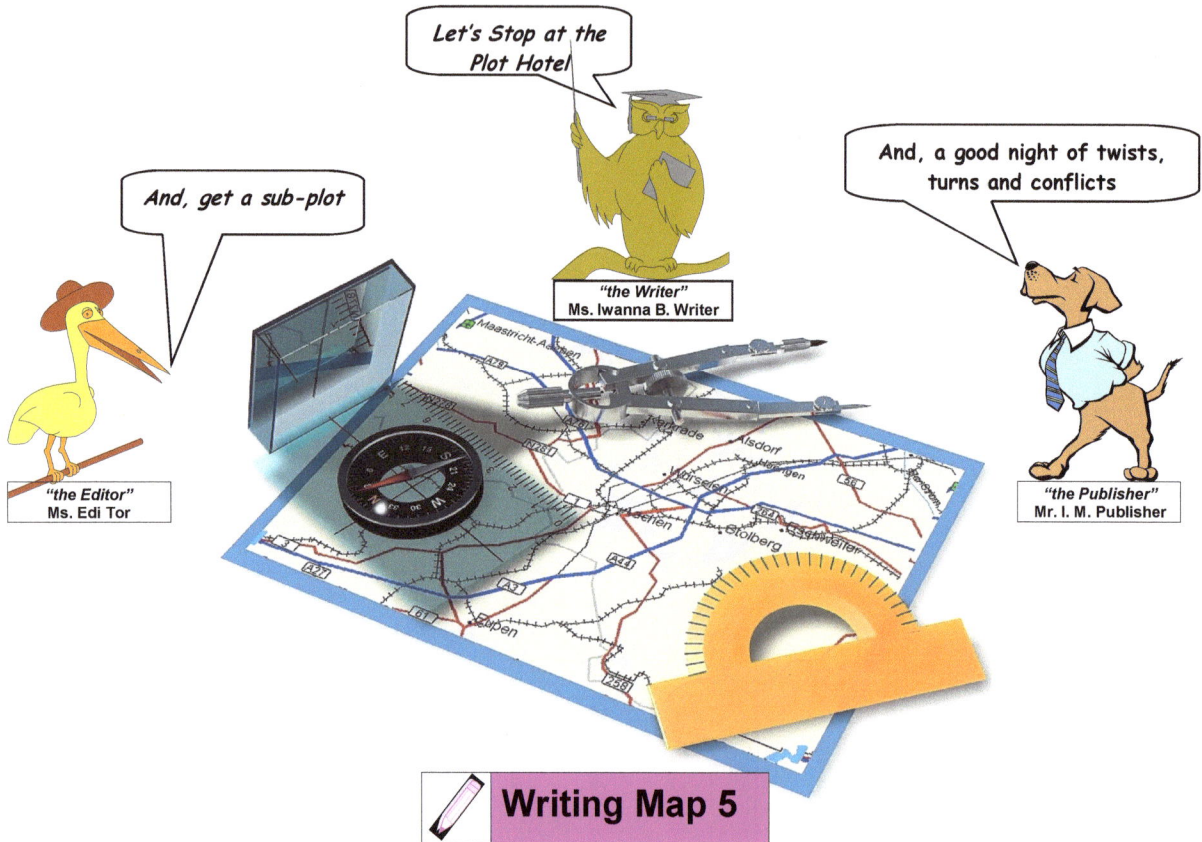

GETTING ON THE ROAD TO YOUR PLOT

Your skeleton has filled out with the flesh of your characters, locations, settings and time periods. Now, we need to add the life line that holds that body together... the plot. The plot is what begins to bring your story to life.

The plot is the blueprint or plan of your story

Plotting is simply the connecting of all the events in your story: the beginning, to a turning point or climax, ending in a resolution. The purpose of plot is to create and control your story idea and all that happens to your characters as the story unfolds.
Readers need a reason to care about your story and to want to keep reading. So you need to create situations that will hold their interest.

Our Guides Agree:

By creating an exciting plot

By creating a well written plot

By creating a plot that satisfies the reader!

Well Devised Plot will accomplish the goals of your story. The plot is the means by which you, the writer: entertain, educate, and satisfy the reader. It's only when there is a clash of forces, and something valuable is at stake, that the reader gets really involved in the story.

17

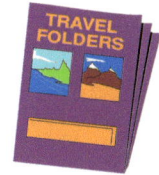

When structuring your plot, go back to your Writing Map 2 Ideas & Outline Form and review the 5 W's information you've already filled in: now we need to use the What, Why and How.

What: What are the issues: conflicts, complications of your story situations ?

Why: Why are these issues important to your story?

How: How are these issues resolved?

> Plot pulls all the pieces to-gether?

There are no magic formulas for writing perfect plots. Plotting involves time and development of what works. There are also no infallible rules, but the more you write the easier plotting a story becomes.

Maneuvering Down the Road of Conflicts

You can also create various conflicts to move your story along. Most stories revolve around problems the characters must deal with and solve. These problems will help make your characters more exciting and grip the reader. Problems may arise from inner conflicts, or from situations that occur in your story.

Types of Conflicts
- A character's struggle with the external forces of nature—such as an environmental disaster
- A struggle with some force of society
- A struggle with another individual
- A struggle within one's self
- Goals—advancing in a competitive field
- Overcoming obstacles—such as: poverty, social status
- Health – dealing with physical and mental problems
- Life's turning points – dealing with situations from birth to death
- Motivation and Desire—achievements; winning and losing

> Humans Love Conflicts !

Example: Bob, a welder for over 40 years was dreading his 60th birthday. That's the day he will be forced to take early retirement.

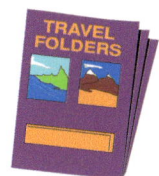

Twists and Turns

Authors often discover when they begin writing a story that their characters determine the direction the story takes. Good! Listen to your characters. If you understand who they are—their hopes, dreams, goals, conflicts, you will soon find them taking on a life of their own. You may have intended a character to react to a problem in a certain way, then realize that character might do it differently. Many authors experiment with plot twists and turns and throw in surprises when they want to help pace the story. But, remember readers are savvy – so, keep your twists and turns believable.

> **Example:** "Remy, how...is this possible? I know you were dead!"
> "No, mon ami. I was kidnapped and held prisoner all these years. My capture and reported death were contrived to prevent us from revealing to the world the greatest discovery in recent history."

Get your Writing Map 5 **PLOT DETAILING** Form from your Travel Kit at the back of this chapter. Using Example #3 write about your **TWISTS & TURNS**

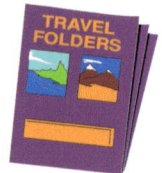

Subplots

Subplots are used to support the major story line or theme and to add interest and intrigue. A subplot is a secondary story line or thread related to the main story line. Subplots are interwoven into the action of a story to create connections and complications. Suspense can be created by having several story lines interweaving at the same time. You could consider a love triangle, a test of courage, a power play, or a sacrifice or redemption plot line. You are limited only by your imagination.

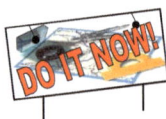

Get your Writing Map 5 **PLOT DETAILING** Form from your Travel Kit at the back of this chapter. Using Example #4 write about your **SUB-PLOT**

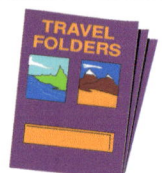

Flash Forward/Foreshadowing

The flash forward takes the reader to an event before it happens
> **Example:** Evie finished her design and signed her name. Her upcoming show would be so successful, her parents would finally agree she could pursue a career in fashion, instead of becoming a scientist, like them.

Fore-shadowing is another device that prepares the reader for an event to come, without giving away specific details.

> **Example:** Brian sees Mrs. MixMatcher give Jonathan a coin. He suspects Controller's using the coin to control Jonathan. The BREV Force later discover the coin was how Controller drove Jonathan crazy.

Flashbacks

Flashbacks are useful to help fill in details of something that happened in the past. When you tell about past events, if you want to show your characters interacting with action and dialogue, flashbacks need to be written as scenes.

> **Example:** Had it really been 20 years since I met Remy at the Scientist Convention. We talked like two old friends until I learned he was the world's youngest Nobel Prize Winner. That moment changed my life.

Flashbacks/forwards or foreshadowing should only be used when useful to your story.

Get your Writing Map 5 **PLOT DETAILING** Form from your Travel Kit at the back of this chapter. Using Example #5 write about your **FLASH FORWARD/FORESHADOWING/FLASH BACK**

Plot Formulas

Plots have unlimited possibilities, but there are basic formulas that help you get from point A to point B in your story.

Suspense, Success or Dream Goal
Before the main character can achieve his goal, he must overcome obstacles. There's suspense, action, intrigue, and the character may or may not achieve his goal.

> **Example:** Brad felt Quiz Master attaching something to this head. He knew if he got out of this alive, he would never again go up against Controller alone. He finally realized his role in The BREV Force.

Love and Relationships
One of the oldest and most varied plot formulas.

> **Example:** Jonathan knew he was a nerd and that Evie was out of his class. She was so beautiful, and he loved her so much. He told himself if he could just be around her, maybe she'd fall in love with him.

The Triangle
This is seen in a struggle of two characters for the affection or loyalty of another. This formula, like the love formula, is often used in romance fiction.

> **Example**: Evie knew she was falling in love with Rick. But she also knew he was rich, gorgeous fast and free...but worse than that he was Sheila's boyfriend.

Redemption:
This involves a change in the character's personality or circumstances.

> **Example**: Jonathan sat facing Evie. He had lied about the coin, lied about Mrs. MixMatcher. Now he was still lying. Evie was crying and couldn't take anymore. No matter what the consequences, he knew he had to come clean.

Sacrifice:

The sacrifice is seen when the character gives up something dear, even his life for a good cause.

Example: Brad knew he was wrong to go out on his own and try to destroy Controller. He'd made so many mistakes. Now he knew what he had to do. He would volunteer for the deadly mission.

Success, Love, Sacrifice— Readers Love It

Get your Writing Map 5 **PLOT DETAILING** Form from your Travel Kit at the back of this chapter. Using Example #6 write about your **PLOT FORMULAS**

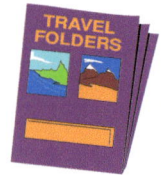

Plotting the Course

When you know exactly where you're story is headed you will be better able to lead the reader down the roads you choose; roads with conflicts, sub-plots and distractions, and those that lead straight to your destination. Plot Detailing helps you when you begin to write. A simple tool to use to make the plot move is to DELIVER a great story!

USE

THE **DELIVER** FORMULA

Devise a problem or issue that exists or is anticipated

Enhance your story by adding complications

Lead to a problem that needs to be solved

Instigate a crisis to overcome

Verbalize dialogue to add realism to a scene

Erupt into a climax

Resolve the problem or issue one way or another

Send your Plot to the Director

Before you even begin writing plot you should be sure you've created one that will be memorable. Think of your favorite movie—and then imagine the whole story taking place around your plot.   Now think of a scene from your favorite book. Can you close your eyes and picture how the story would unfold?

A well written plot is what we want you to achieve, so don't skimp on any details. Sometimes the most insignificant plots lead to a great story that leaves a lasting impression.

The best way to check if you have created a viable plot, including sub-plots, conflicts, twists and turns, is to go back to your — Writing Map 5 Plot Detailing Form, and look over the details. Ask yourself whether or not a Director could take your information and know exactly how to make your story into a movie.

Play Director and send your plot to the movies—

What would the advertising slogan be?

_____

_____

What would the trailer(promotional piece) include? _____

_____

What one scene would best describe your story? _____

_____

Have a question about Plot? e-mail tech support at:

info@goldenquillpress.com Subject: How To Write Your Book—question Plot

Writing Map 5

TRIP REVIEW
Map Directions

Plot Makes Your Skeleton Into A Fashionably Dressed Traveler
Stopping For A Bit Of Conflict Makes For A Better Entertained Reader
Every Road Should Lead To The Resolution

Travel Instructions — Did You?

❐   Do your Plot Detailing
     Add Plot Detailing to your

❐   Send your Plot to the Director

OUR GUIDES
Point You In The Right Direction

Plot out your plot—
Wh—Wh--what was
that story about?

A bird in the
hand—tells one
heck of a story!

That great plot even
kept the barking
dogs quiet

◀ NOTE ▶
There's no magic formula for writing perfect plots, but the more you read and the more
you practice writing, the better storyteller you will become.

Writing Map 5 | PLOT DETAILING | Travel Kit Form

Example Plot Detailing

#1 Main Plot: Computer virus, Controller, headquartered in Island Falls is trying to take over the world. Each member of the Kane Family is working to destroy Controller.

#2 Conflict: Martin and Vivian are working as fast as they can to find an antidote to Controller but time is running out — their children are getting ready to face-off with the computer virus and its holograms

#3 Twists and Turns: Brad tries to save Jonathan and he is captured by Quiz Master and Controller. Evie, Jonathan and Rick try to save Brad and wind up in Controller's love triangle.

#4 Sub-Plot: In order to save their friends from Controller Evie and Brad's experiments turn them into super beings

#5 Flash Forward/Foreshadow: Martin is stuck in traffic. He wishes he'd phoned Vivian before he left the Cottage. He smiles as he envisions entering their house; she appears at the door as beautiful as the day they met over 20 years before. But a dark cloud intrudes on his thoughts, *How will I tell her about the stranger's visit and her threat to our lives?*

#5a Flash Back: Martin took the notebook from his secret drawer. The sight of the now tattered black book that contained their cloning formula, thrust him back more than 20 years to the day his life changed; he met Dr. Remy Marcel

#6 Plot Formula: Controller has threatened college students. Martin and Vivian are ordered to find the way to destroy it; while their children and their clone prepare to do battle with the entity and its holograms: Cracko, Quiz Master and MixMatcher.

Your Plot Detailing

Main Plot: _____

Conflict: _____

Twists and Turns: _____

Sub-Plot: _____

Flash Forward/Foreshadow _____

Flash Back: _____

Plot Formula: _____

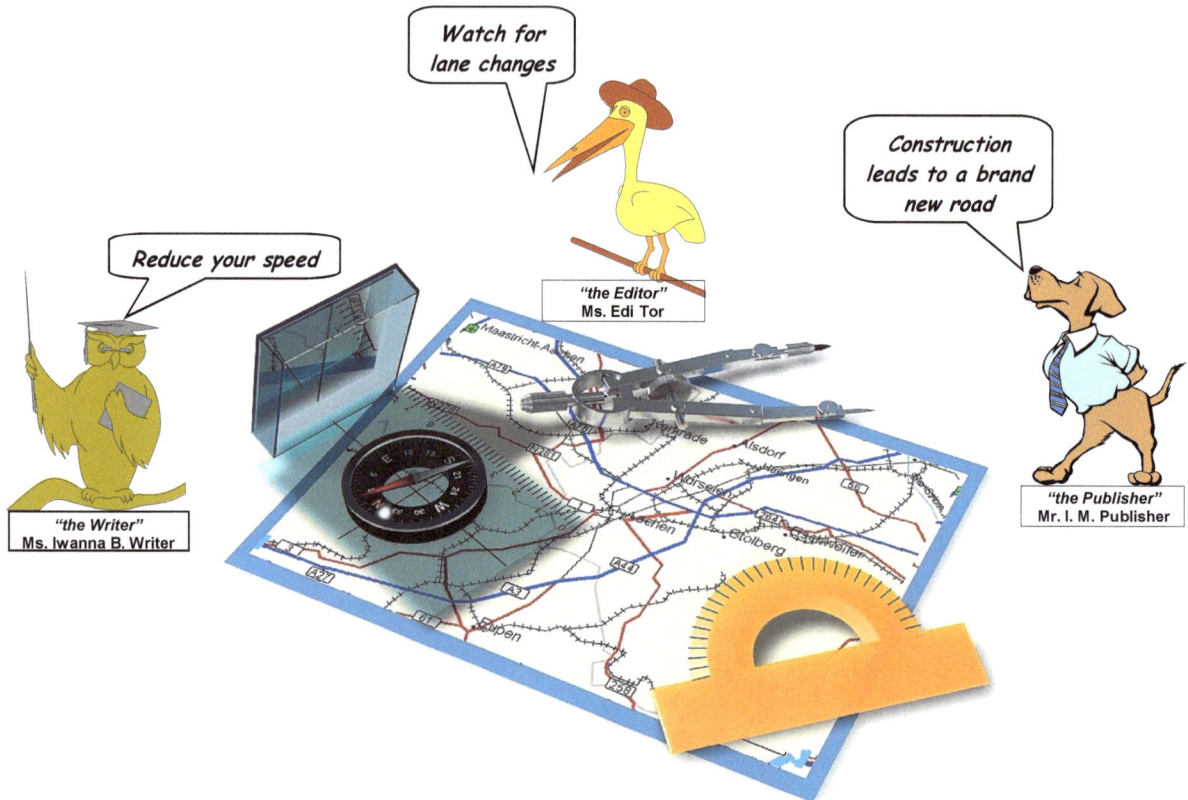

Watch for lane changes

Reduce your speed

Construction leads to a brand new road

"the Editor"
Ms. Edi Tor

"the Writer"
Ms. Iwanna B. Writer

"the Publisher"
Mr. I. M. Publisher

Writing Map 6

CONSTRUCTING YOUR STORY

Now that we have all the major elements of your story we're ready to enter our Construction zone.

Structuring Your Story

As with all construction zones we need to take it slow and watch out for caution signs. Getting you safely through this section will take our journey onto a newly paved road. Some writers find, getting those first few words down on paper, the most difficult part of writing. To get you through this complex area, we'll use information we discovered in our workshops. Writers who used our "Detailing Forms," had a better grip on their ideas and easily found their way through the constructing process.

Your Story Beginning

As with all things we must begin at the Beginning. When you read the first few pages of a book, notice how the author begins. Look for ideas that hold your interest and draw you into the story. It could be a setting, a character or a plot, but whatever it is – it Hooks YOU! . And, so it's called, "The Hook."

SLOW

25

It's an essential part of writing a book. A hook can be almost anything from a question that must be answered—to a shock scene that leaves the reader wanting more. You can build a place and time that is so fascinating the reader wants to visit often, or you can begin with a love or hate character. Sometimes just mentioning a situation and then leaving it at that, can really make a reader want to hitch hike along with you. Whatever type of hook you choose, your story beginning should incorporate that hook. Be sure you make it strong enough to arouse interest and hold the reader's attention.

Writers catch more fish with a GREAT HOOK!

Example: Controller, a computer virus has invaded Island Falls and is using this college town's vulnerable young people to achieve it's goals of taking over the world.

Establish Your Hook

 My Hook is

_____

_____

_____

Onto the Play

Once you've established your "Hook," the next step is to weave it into your story. When you begin to write, it's helpful to visualize how your story will unfold. Just as a play has three acts; stories need to have three segments that divide the action: a beginning, a middle and an end.

The first segment will be the Opening Act: that's where you place your "Hook." This beginning part leads the reader into the story; arouses interest, and holds their attention with the "Hook." This first act should also: introduce the characters, establish the setting, and set the mood and tone of the story.

When the curtain rises on Act II the story should have progressed to the middle. This is where most of the excitement, conflict and intrigue are centered. The tensions should build as the suspense grips the audience and keeps the anticipation high until the curtain falls. This part may take about one half or more of your manuscript to develop. Remember to pace the action; don't put everything in the middle.

The last act is called Resolution. This is the act in which: events and situations are solved, conclusions are reached, loose ends are tied up and any remaining problems are resolved. The outcome or clarification of the plot in a story is called the denouement. Like the final act in a play; when the curtain falls, the audience should be left with a satisfied feeling; the time was enjoyable, understandable and well spent.

Your story can end on a happy or sad note, but it should leave the reader satisfied—not feeling cheated, confused or disappointed. And always remember to tie up all the loose ends. Nothing turns a reader off more than an incomplete ending.

When the end of your story leaves the reader with a flash of insight or a sense of understanding, it is called an epiphany ending. Surprise endings are also effective. Just when the reader thinks the story has come to an end—something exciting happens that creates another crisis. We will discuss beginnings and endings in more detail later.

The following diagram that resembles a stage can be a guide to structuring your story.

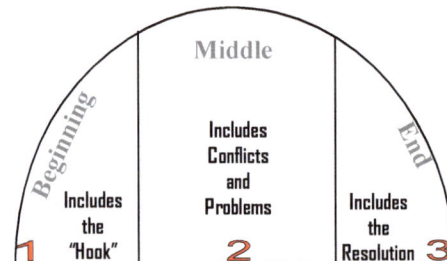

Caught up in Traffic

Converting your ideas into your first draft can be as frustrating as being on a one-lane construction road. You want to get going, but you have to go slow and stay in line. There are many ways to begin this task, but our workshops have provided three techniques that were very helpful to writers: Clustering, Outlining and Story Boarding.
Look over all three and then decide which will work best for you.
First, let's exit at the Drive-In to see how this works.

Let's Go to the Drive-In Movie

If you've ever been to a drive-in movie you know it's basically a big empty parking lot with a huge size movie screen. Well, for our purposes we're going to use that setting to visualize sitting in your car at the drive-in and watching your story unfold on the screen. Visualization is the main key to clustering, outlining or storyboarding. So, get comfortable, relax and get ready to enjoy a great movie — Yours!
First be sure there are no distractions — visualize the drive-in as if you're attending a private screening of your story. Sit back and take some slow deep breaths and clear your mind. Then close your eyes and watch your movie in your mind's eye. The music comes on – the credits appear on the screen and then your story begins.
Allow your thoughts to carry you along as you watch. Trust your instincts — it's your story — without pushing you'll be able to travel from scene to scene. Your story will be shown in chronological order. In many cases, you might want your story to start with a flashback or scene that is disconnected, but for the purposes of our movie, your story will run chronologically.
As you watch the very beginning stop and jot down a few words about what you're seeing. Now return to your visualization and stop at the next major scene. Do the same for every <u>major</u> scene from beginning to end, (you will fill in details later, for now just concentrate on the most important events of your story). Now you should have enough information to begin your story construction. Our Guides want to produce your movie, but they have limited funds. Every scene must be vital to the storyline. Be sure each scene: either develops a character, introduces an element of the story or in some

way moves the story along. If not, throw it out. When you're sure you have all the major scenes, let the drive-in movie run again. Watch the story completely in your mind and let the details begin to fill in. Let the story take on a life of it's own and see where it goes. You may find new characters, settings, and plot twists and turns you didn't think of originally.

Now let's see which method of construction works best for you: (SELECT ONLY ONE)

Choice 1: Clustering through Traffic

Clustering means gathering together and we're going to gather your characters, plots and sub-plots, settings etc., so we can visualize how your story will put flesh on the skeleton. We recommend one Clustering Form for each stage: Beginning, Middle and End.

Get your Writing Map 6 **Beginning Cluster Detailing** Form from your Travel Kit at the back of this chapter, then follow the instructions below.

Start with your Hook. Put it in the center box. Then decide what events, or elements are most important to the beginning of the story and how they will intersect with the Hook. Write one word in each circle.

Choice 2: Outlining your way Around

Another way to gather your story together is to outline. Outlining involves writing a simple sentence for each scene and interconnecting them. Go back to Map 2 your "From Idea to Outline Form." Use your original outline and embellish each scene to cover your beginning and then do the same for the middle and end.

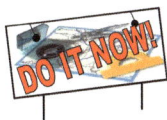

Get your Writing Map 6 **Beginning Outline Detailing** Form from your Travel Kit at the back of this chapter.

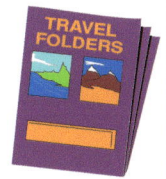

Choice 3: Stopping at the Beach for some Storyboarding

Storyboarding is a technique used in the movies and television to lay out the scenes to be filmed.   It's a series of pictures and/or notes arranged to chart the flow of the story. In writing we use a similar storyboard to lay out the major sequences from beginning to end. A storyboard will give you a visual picture of how your story unfolds and connects Chapter to Chapter. If you already have your story written you can use storyboarding to check continuity and review scenes: for pacing, plot twist, character development and sometimes even to change how the scene unravels. To use story-boarding you will need either index cards, (white and colors), a chalkboard and white and colored chalk, or large oak tag (also called poster board) and colored pencils. You'll also need to set up an area that allows you to view your scenes in a continuous manner — for index cards, pin or tape them to an empty wall, corkboard or on a large oak tag/poster board.

NOTE: Our Writing Guides Suggest:

THE INDEX CARD SYSTEM IS THE SIMPLEST METHOD. FOR OUR PURPOSES OUR EXAMPLE WILL USE THIS SYSTEM.

Start with approximately 20 white index cards. Each card will represent a major scene. Either draw or jot down enough information to visually depict that scene.

Next, take your colored index cards and write the filler that leads each scene to the next. Your colored index card # 1A would fill in the interim events between Card #1 and Card #2. You can also expand your storyboarding to include vital information. One color for other main character's, one color for sub-plots. Soon, you will see a pattern. The white cards may represent chapters and the colored ones the details that take you from one chapter to the next.

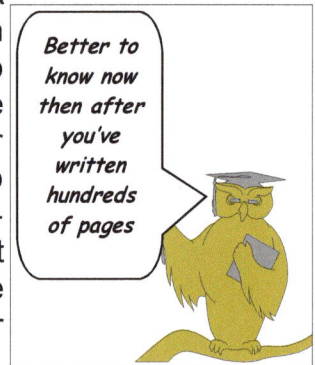

The hardest thing for a writer to admit is that every scene isn't a gem

Better to know now then after you've written hundreds of pages

EXAMPLE: Index card #1 A woman mysteriously arrives at Martin's office and orders him to work for the government.

Index card #2 Martin hides papers in his home office which contain the illegal experiments he's secretly been working on.

Index card # 1A On his drive home Martin pictures his pregnant wife and decides not to tell her the details of the papers in his briefcase.

Our Writing Guides Suggest:

We know you are eager to begin writing, but there's still a great deal of information that will assist you in writing your first draft — that will save you time in editing and revising – so be patient and you will be rewarded.

SAMPLE Storyboarding Diagram to assist you with what your final story-boarding should look like.

Code: **White -** major scenes — **Yellow-** character info
Gold- Subplots — **Blue-** important info to interject

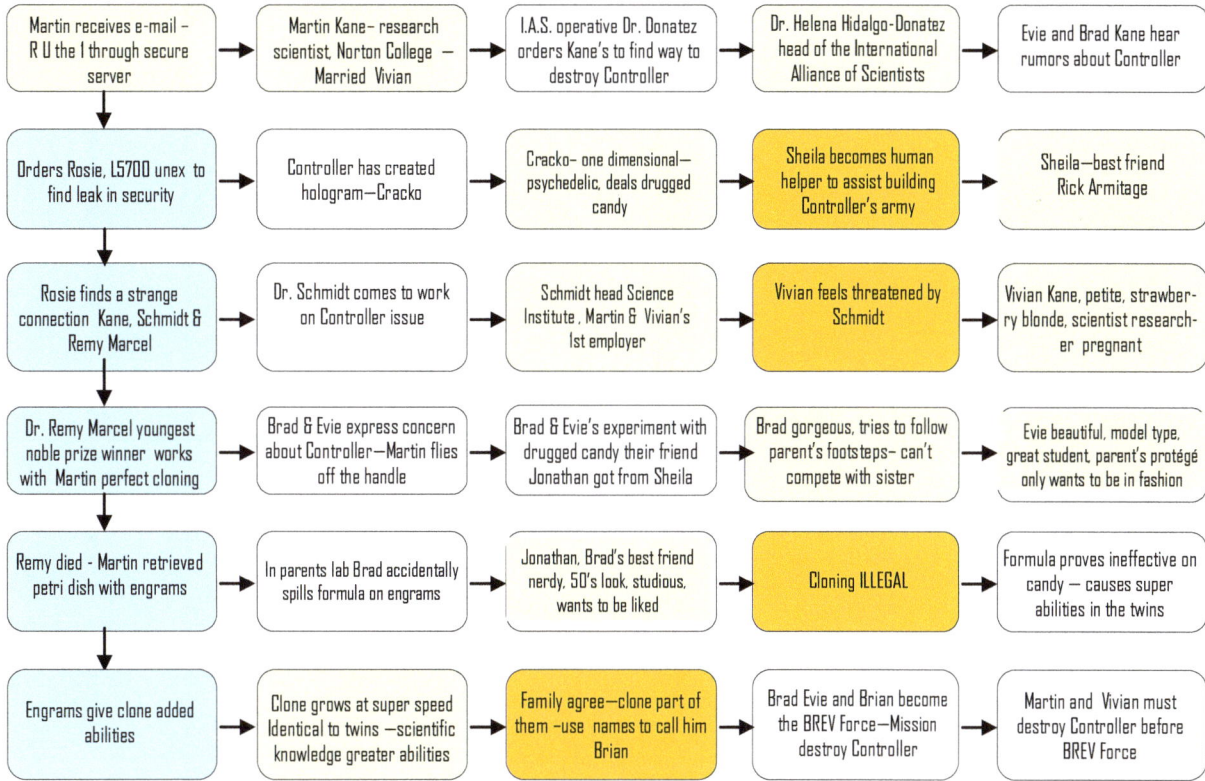

Martin receives e-mail – R U the I through secure server	Martin Kane– research scientist, Norton College — Married Vivian	I.A.S. operative Dr. Donatez orders Kane's to find way to destroy Controller	Dr. Helena Hidalgo-Donatez head of the International Alliance of Scientists	Evie and Brad Kane hear rumors about Controller
Orders Rosie, L5700 unex to find leak in security	Controller has created hologram—Cracko	Cracko- one dimensional—psychedelic, deals drugged candy	Sheila becomes human helper to assist building Controller's army	Sheila—best friend Rick Armitage
Rosie finds a strange connection Kane, Schmidt & Remy Marcel	Dr. Schmidt comes to work on Controller issue	Schmidt head Science Institute, Martin & Vivian's 1st employer	Vivian feels threatened by Schmidt	Vivian Kane, petite, strawberry blonde, scientist researcher pregnant
Dr. Remy Marcel youngest noble prize winner works with Martin perfect cloning	Brad & Evie express concern about Controller—Martin flies off the handle	Brad & Evie's experiment with drugged candy their friend Jonathan got from Sheila	Brad gorgeous, tries to follow parent's footsteps– can't compete with sister	Evie beautiful, model type, great student, parent's protégé only wants to be in fashion
Remy died - Martin retrieved petri dish with engrams	In parents lab Brad accidentally spills formula on engrams	Jonathan, Brad's best friend nerdy, 50's look, studious, wants to be liked	Cloning ILLEGAL	Formula proves ineffective on candy — causes super abilities in the twins
Engrams give clone added abilities	Clone grows at super speed Identical to twins —scientific knowledge greater abilities	Family agree—clone part of them —use names to call him Brian	Brad Evie and Brian become the BREV Force—Mission destroy Controller	Martin and Vivian must destroy Controller before BREV Force

Free Writing

FREE as a Bird - Works for Me

Once you've maneuvered through the miles of construction, your next traffic slow up will be Free Writing. The purpose of Free Writing is to take your Clustering, Outline, or Story Board and convert it to the written word. Free writing is connecting the dots with words. Short burst of words or thoughts connect the Hook to your story's beginning. Free writing is whatever comes into your mind; you don't get stopped by punctuation, dialogue or in depth description, and the only rule in this session is stick to the Clustering, Outline or Story Board. This is your way to cross the bridge from ideas to actual writing, without having to worry about the formalities. This bridge doesn't have a toll and it takes your vehicle from a one-lane constructed road to a three lane written highway.

Get your Writing Map 6 *Free Writing Detailing* Form and your *Beginning Cluster/Outline or Story Board Detailing* Form from your Travel Kit at the back of this chapter.

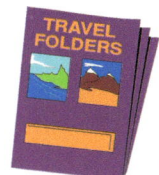

Don't forget to use each point. You may also find that as you begin to write you may add other factors that had never occurred to you before.

Are you feeling a Draft

Now, we are ready to take your Free Writing and turn it into your first draft. Here are some tips to help you prepare. Use these keys to start your writing engine:

The words often called keys to good writing begin with "C."

CLEAR	**CONCISE**	**CONSISTENT**
CORRECT	**COMPLETE**	**CONSCIENTIOUS**
	CONTINUITY	

"C's" Keys
1 Mile

CLEAR -
The English language has been developing for centuries and new words are added every day. Unless you're writing a period piece, try to use words your readers will understand. Always say exactly what you mean. Let's examine clichés; those old expressions can sometimes clutter a writer's work. Here are a few:

Example:

Last but not least	Smart as a whip	Clear as a crystal
Music to my ears	Cool as a cucumber	Pretty as a picture
Raining cats and dogs	Easy as pie	Sharp as a tack

There are hundreds of clichés. Don't let them dull your writing. Choose words that are fresh and expressive.

CONCISE -
Conciseness in writing means to write without using long words (several syllables) when a simple word will do.

Example: Incorrect – "I'm going to my residence, then I'm going to retire."
This sentence is wordy and pretentious. It'd be better to say:
Correct – "I'm going home, then I'm going to bed."

CONSISTENT -
Means to stay within the same tense

Example: Incorrect – "We went to visit a friend, but she is not there."
This sentence shifts from past tense (was) to present tense (is).
Correct – "We went to visit a friend, but she was not (wasn't) there."

Number and Person.
Example: Incorrect – "We went to a play one knew would be dull."
This sentence shifts from first person plural (we) to third person singular (one).
Correct: - "We went to a play we knew would be dull."

COMPLETE -

When telling a story, it's important to include facts the reader would not know. Remember the reader is not in your head so spell it out! Use specific words for clarity.

Example: Incorrect –"She was angry, she picked up something and threw it."
The sentence did not indicate who was angry; what item she picked up or why she threw it.
Correct – "Mary was angry with Tom because he was late for dinner. She picked up an apple and threw it at him."

CONSCIENTIOUS -

Words help to portray different characters through description and dialogue. Language that's appropriate for one character may be all wrong for another. For instance, the reader expects the vocabulary of an educated professor to differ from that of a hip teenager.

Example: (Professor) – "I'll examine all the possibilities and get back to you at a later date.
(Teenager) – "Dude, I'll check it out and ketch ya later."

Conscientious writing also examines character gender. Try not using "He" when a job is done by men and women. Writers often solve this problem by using gender free writing: Barbara is the new mailperson.

To avoid gender-specific language, try these suggestions:

Instead of:	Use Gender-free Writing:
Mankind	People
Salesman	Salesperson or Representative
Businessman	Executive or businessperson
Foreman	Supervisor
Fireman	Firefighter
Workman	Worker

CORRECT –

Finally, read through your work line by line searching for errors in punctuation, spelling, structure and over all clarity. Use pronouns and nouns instead of starting a sentence with "IT" or "THAT."

CONTINUITY—

One of the most important aspects of any story is continuity. Keeping your facts straight and always making sure you know where everyone and everything should be at all times.

Example: Martin searches frantically for his lost keys and finally finds them on the small table in the hallway. He shakes his head, *How could I have missed seeing them they were the only object on the table*.

(Next scene)   Rushing out the door, Martin looks around for his keys and finally spots them; glittering next to a heavy glass ashtray.
If the keys were the only object on the table, then how could they be glittering next to the heavy ashtray?

32

CONTINUITY CONT'D —

Example: Brad put on his <u>blue suit</u> in preparation for his court appearance.

(Next scene) When Brad is introduced to the District Attorney, he shakes hands then removes his <u>grey jacket</u>.

How can Brad be wearing a blue suit with a jacket that's grey?

Facts are so important to keep straight — so don't let the reader catch you being Incontinent-- Oh Inconsistent

Example: Martin went downstairs and signaled the code that unlocked the secret laboratory. <u>He entered and closed the interior door</u>.

Next scene) Martin heard the "intruder alert" and <u>ran out of the lab and up stairs</u> to the building entrance.

Martin never opened the interior door to go upstairs

Well, by now we're sure you are experts on the "C's," so now it's time to park your car for the night and take a well deserved rest— some "Z's."

The next step of your trip will be writing your first draft!

Writing Map 6

TRIP REVIEW
Map Directions

Clustering, Outlining & Story Boarding Keep Track of How Your Story Will Evolve

Free Writing Speeds You Through The Construction Zone

Drafts Are The Vehicle That Road Tests Your Story

Travel Instructions — Did You?

- ❏ Do Clustering/Outline/Story Boarding
- ❏ Do Free Writing
- ❏ Add the forms to your
- ❏ Remember the "C's" Keys

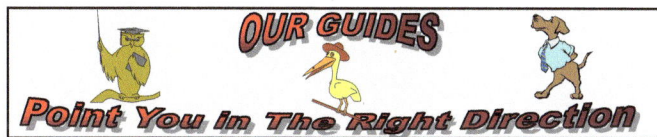

OUR GUIDES Point You in The Right Direction

Your Great Hook might even Catch an OWL!!

Writing Free as a Bird is a Great Way to Get Started

First Draft—Second - Third - keep barking up that tree 'til you get it right

◀ **NOTE** ▶
Following all the road maps and taking your time through the Detailing, Clustering/ Outlining/Story Boarding and Free Writing will save time when you begin writing your Drafts.

BEGINNING CLUSTER DETAILING **Form**

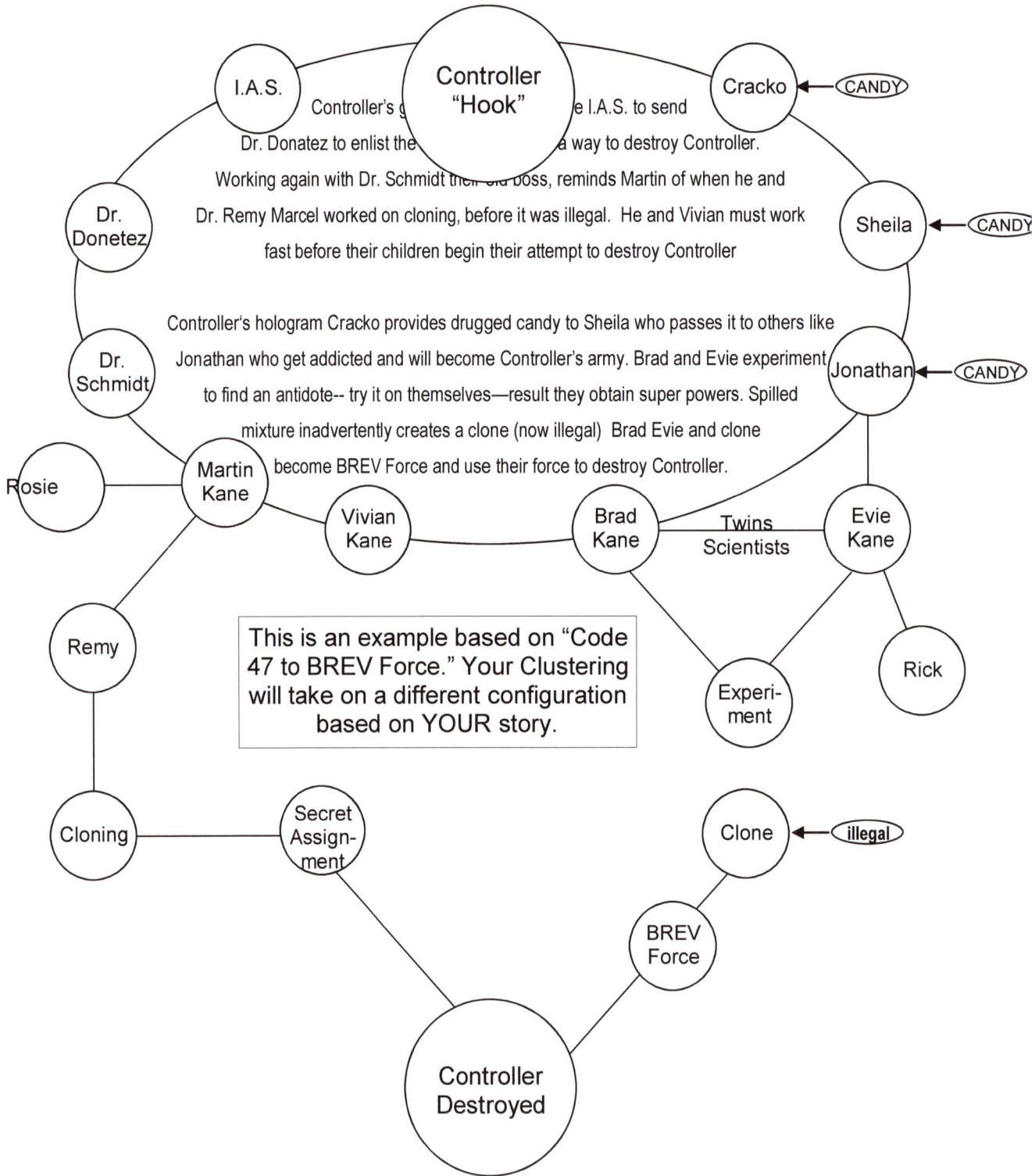

I.A.S.

Controller "Hook"

Cracko — CANDY

Controller's g... ...e I.A.S. to send Dr. Donatez to enlist the ... a way to destroy Controller. Working again with Dr. Schmidt their old boss, reminds Martin of when he and Dr. Remy Marcel worked on cloning, before it was illegal. He and Vivian must work fast before their children begin their attempt to destroy Controller

Dr. Donetez

Sheila — CANDY

Controller's hologram Cracko provides drugged candy to Sheila who passes it to others like Jonathan who get addicted and will become Controller's army. Brad and Evie experiment to find an antidote-- try it on themselves—result they obtain super powers. Spilled mixture inadvertently creates a clone (now illegal) Brad Evie and clone become BREV Force and use their force to destroy Controller.

Dr. Schmidt

Jonathan — CANDY

Rosie

Martin Kane

Vivian Kane

Brad Kane

Twins Scientists

Evie Kane

Remy

Rick

Experi- ment

This is an example based on "Code 47 to BREV Force." Your Clustering will take on a different configuration based on YOUR story.

Cloning

Secret Assign- ment

Clone — illegal

BREV Force

Controller Destroyed

Writing Map 6

BEGINNING OUTLINE DETAILING

Form

EXAMPLE: Original OUTLINE	Your Original OUTLINE :

EXAMPLE: Original OUTLINE

A computer virus has grown beyond its original programming and has invaded the small college town of Island Falls. Controller has programmed holograms to do its bidding and to persuade college students to join its ranks.

Scientists Martin and Vivian Kane are recruited to stop Controller. Their children's (Brad and Evie) best friend, Jonathan, becomes hooked by Controller's forces (hologram Cracko and human helper Sheila) and Brad and Evie strike out on their own to defeat Controller.

Your Original OUTLINE :

_____
_____
_____
_____
_____
_____
_____

EXAMPLE: Story Beginning OUTLINE

Controller, a computer virus has grown beyond its original programming and become more than a virus –

Headquartered in Island Falls, a 2 college town, gives Controller a lot of possible recruits for its evil.

Uses holograms, first one – Cracko—like a drug dealer—and Sheila, human convert to deal out mind altering drugged candies.

The I.A.S. an international scientific agency has been monitoring this computer phenomenon.
They send Dr. Donatez to persuade the Kanes (Martin and Vivian) to develop a way to destroy Controller
They will be happy to be working again with their old boss, Dr. Schmidt. It has been years and that reminds Martin of when he met Dr. Remy Marcel and worked on cloning. It was legal then

Brad and Evie Kane's friend Jonathan is one of Controller's recruits.
Fearing for his life, they use their scientific knowledge to try and find an antidote to the drugged candy.
Brad and Evie experiment to find an antidote
They try it on themselves first
It gives them super abilities.
Some of the formula spilled and inadvertently created a clone.
Cloning is now illegal.
Brad Evie and clone become BREV Force and vow to destroy Controller.

Martin and Vivian must work fast to find the way to destroy Controller, before their children face off with it.

Your Story Beginning OUTLINE :

_____
_____
_____
_____
_____
_____
_____
_____
_____
_____
_____
_____
_____
_____
_____
_____
_____
_____
_____
_____
_____
_____
_____

Writing Map 6 · FREE WRITING DETAILING · Form

Example Free Writing Detailing

Martin opened his e-mail

< "R U the 1" >

"somehow I've been *targeted for this garbage, but how?"*

e-mail account maintained through a high level security server SPAM factors set at highest priority security level password protected code was necessary for incoming mail also an auto blocker for any non verified e-mails. world's most secure server? Order ROSIE *find out how it gets through and where its coming from*

New Homeland Security warning from General Babcok website, www.natsecurity.classified.gov set up list suspected terrorist

Kane's ordered to work with Dr. Schmidt to destroy Controller by Dr. Helena Hidalgo Donatez of ISA

Martin calls General Babcock and then the President

Controller invades Island Falls campuses hologram Cracko turns students into loyal army

Jonathan becomes follower— Brad and Evie experiment — clone created and super powers— go up against Controller and Cracko

Your Free Writing Detailing

Who's telling the story?

I'm telling the story--

No! Mr. Spaniel is telling the story

"the Writer"
Ms. Iwanna B. Writer

"the Editor"
Ms. Edi Tor

"the Publisher"
Mr. I. M. Publisher

Writing Map 7

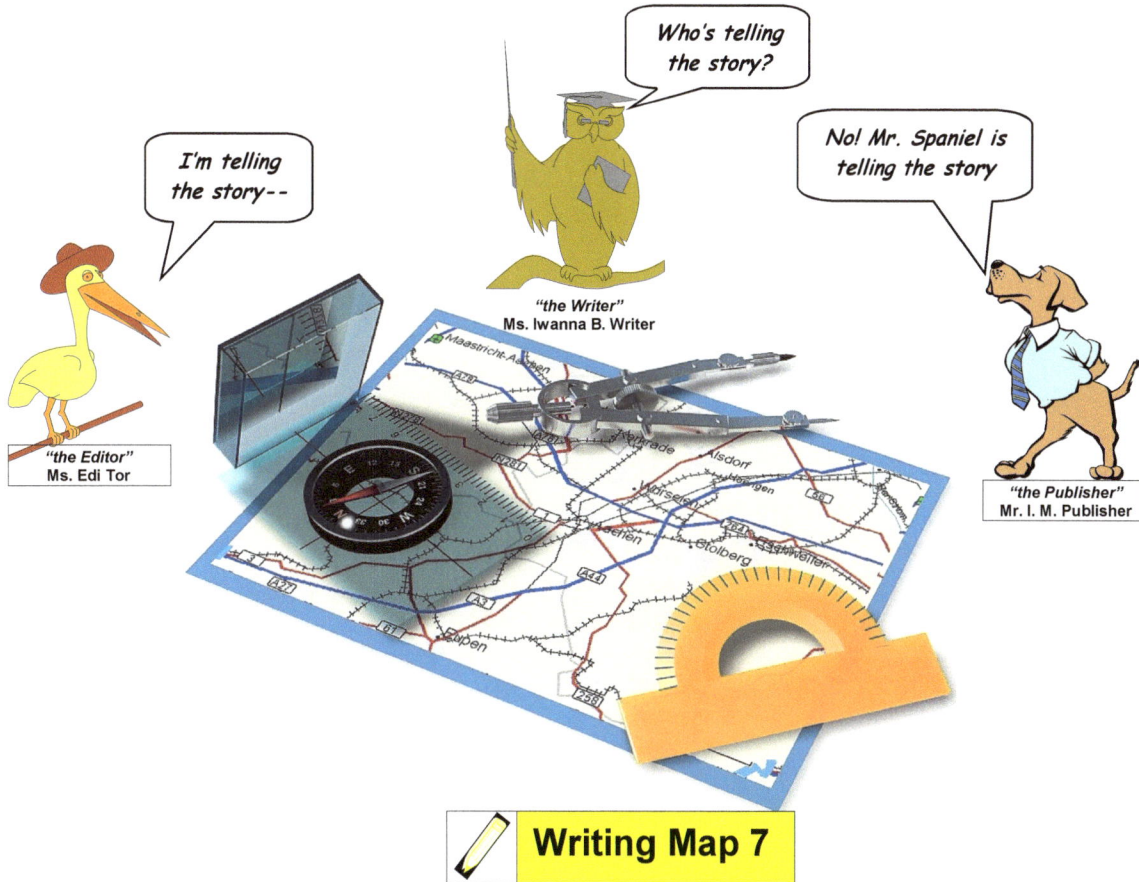

LOOKING THROUGH THE REAR VIEW MIRROR

Before we begin our journey today we need to decide who is going to drive. As the narrator, or one who tells or writes the story, you must decide from whose point of view your story will be told. That will be your designated driver .

Choosing your View--point

A story told in the first person uses the pronoun "I" throughout the story. This view-point allows the reader to get into the writer's head or to see through the eyes of the major character. Memoirs and personal experiences, tend to work best when written in the first person.

First Person Viewpoint: <u>The writer tells the story:</u>
    Example: "I remember the first time I met Remy."
        The writer tells the entire story
        from this "I" viewpoint.

Ok, Ok But, Who's point drives the story ?

    The first person viewpoint has its advantages because it allows you to deal with one mind — as if following the events of a story with a camera; relating what you see.

38

A word of caution: the disadvantage of first person viewpoint is that you can't get into the minds of other characters — you're writing what you see, hear, feel, and experience.

First Person Character's Viewpoint: <u>One Character tells the story</u>.
> **Example:** My name is Dr. Helena Hidalgo and the town I come from is Hidalgo Mexico, named for my ancestors.

The main character can't tell you anything from another character's point of view

Second Person Viewpoint: <u>The Who Speaking is "YOU"</u>
Second person viewpoint is where you address the reader directly. It's a difficult, but not impossible concept; generally not recommended for first time novelists.
> **Example:** When **you're** sound asleep in the middle of the night, and the telephone rings, **you** wonder who could be calling.

Second Person Viewpoint <u>Used in non-fiction, "How-to" articles, and recipes</u>
> **Example:** **You** need 4 ripe tomatoes, 2 small onions and 1 teaspoon of salt. **You** blend all ingredients...and so on.

Third Person Viewpoint: <u>Through the eyes of many characters.</u>
Third Person Viewpoint is told through the eyes of one character at a time. The narrator knows the thoughts, experiences and feelings of that character and all the other characters and when speaking uses the **characters name** or "**he**" or "**she**." No matter how many characters tell their viewpoint, the entire story should be told in third person.

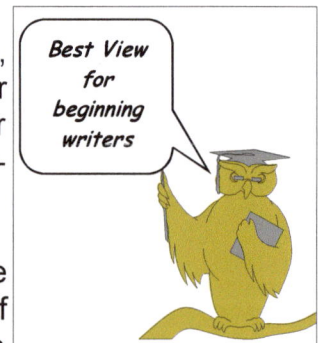

Best View for beginning writers

> **Example:** Martin walked back into his main office. He was bewildered by the odd events of Dr. Donatez's mysterious arrival, "Rosie, pull up her 'Oneness' information, I want to check her security clearance."

Point Your reader to the Right View.

(another character's point of view)
"I'm way ahead of you," she replied, "so I did some additional checking. But, other than her 'Oneness,' all information is classified top secret, 'Eyes Only'." She thought for a moment — *maybe I'll just hack my way in!*
(When the character speaks the character says "I")

As the story unfolds, we follow the characters through the eyes of the narrator. We see what they say, do and think and how they relate to others in the story. Third person viewpoint is often favored by beginning writers because it's easy to control.

Choosing a viewpoint depends on the kind of story you're writing. If you want to tell the story as if you are experiencing the events, choose first person. When you want to interact with all the characters, use third person viewpoint.

There are also more advanced and complex viewpoints, such as:

Third Person Limited Viewpoint: <u>Limited to One Character</u>

> **Example:** Evie ran as fast as she could toward the main campus where her car was parked. She got in and locked the door. She was shaking. *Why was Brad acting that way?* A knock on her window scared her half to death. "Brad!" she screamed, opening the window and holding her heart, "You could've killed me!"
>
> "What's wrong with you? I saved you!" he said.

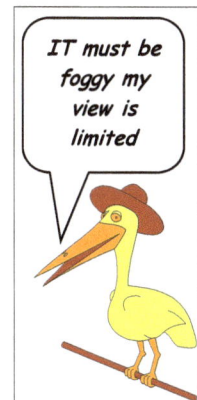

The third person limited viewpoint is widely used by authors, especially in short stories. This viewpoint limits the narrator to the feelings, experiences and thoughts of only one character. That character can, however, draw out the thoughts, feelings and ideas other characters express through the use of dialogue.

Third Person Omniscient Viewpoint allows the author to tell the story as if he's watching it unfold. This is often called the <u>"God" viewpoint.</u> <u>The narrator sees all, knows all, and can take the reader anywhere; in any or all of the character's minds.</u>

In the following, the narrator tells what each character does, thinks, feels and says.

> **Example:** Evie knew Brad was a great researcher and if anyone could figure out what was in that strange candy, he could.
>
> Once inside the lab Brad found the materials he needed to analyze the ingredients of the candy.
>
> Sheila waited outside the lab praying they wouldn't learn the truth.

Now that you know enough ways to point your view

Get your Writing Map 7 **VIEWPOINT DETAILING** Form from your Travel Kit at the back of this chapter decide which point of view works for your story

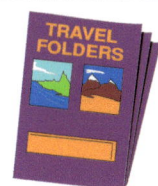

First Draft

You're finally through the construction zone and have your view pointed in the right direction; so now you're ready to get on the super highway of writing. This is the road that turns your Free Writing into your first draft. The draft is the preliminary rough road to your story. Authors often write and rewrite several drafts before they're satisfied with the finished work.

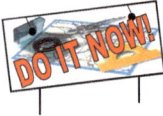

Go back to Your Travel Folder Writing Map #6 and get your *Free Writing Detailing* Form. Read it over and then:

Fill up your tank with your ideas and use them to get back on the road again. Only this time instead of Free Writing: use structured sentences, embellish with description, add dialogue and let's get up to speed. Once you get through the first few Chapters of your first draft you have green lights to continue through that draft to the end of your story.

Your goal is to write your story so it will flow from beginning to end in an entertaining, organized manner. Following this road will lead to some tips for writing sentences, dialogue, description and more in the next few Writing Maps:

Do some "FREE" writing and get feedback. We will post your short story (Maximum 500 Words) on
www.goldenquillpress.com/freewriting.html

Email your post to us for consideration at

info@goldenquillpress.com   subject– How to Write –Free Writing for Feedback

---

So, Let's Start Beginning the Beginning:

Writing Map 7

TRIP REVIEW

Map Directions

First Person Viewpoint Is Often Favored For Non-Fiction "How-to" Books & Articles

Third Person Limited Viewpoint Is Often The Story Tellers Choice

Omniscient Viewpoint Can Be Useful As A Way To Control Your Characters

Travel Instructions — Did You?

☐   Choose Your Viewpoint

☐   Add to your

OUR GUIDES

Point You In The Right Direction

Avoid shifting viewpoints until you have mastered the techniques.

Practice writing stories from different viewpoints.

Read and study how other authors handle viewpoint.

◀ NOTE ▶

Choosing the right viewpoint helps you show and tell your story more effectively.

| ✏️ **Writing Map 7** | VIEWPOINT DETAILING | **Form** |

First Person Viewpoint Detailing
The writer tells the story:

"I remember the first time I met Remy. I never would have imagined he was the youngest noble prize winner.
Character's viewpoint.

My name is Brian Vincent Kane, the name my family gave me when I went to live with them.

Second Person Viewpoint Detailing
Direct to the Reader

When **you're** lying awake in the middle of the night, **you** can hear every sound; every tick of the clock, and rain drop against the window pane.

Third Person Viewpoint Detailing
Character's point of view

Brad's mother, Vivian wanted to cry. She felt all her son's hurts.
(When the character speaks the character says "I")

"I wish you would talk to your father, Brad. Maybe he would understand why you did it. You know I do."

Limited
One Character's View

Evie knew something was wrong. Her emotions were getting in the way and she couldn't reach Brad's mind. **She** decided to try again. "Code 47, Brad please respond?"

Omniscient
Any and all character's views

Brian was sure Controller was still alive and time was running out to prove it.

Brad couldn't help but wonder why Brian was still so obsessed with Controller.

Evie wished she knew what was going on with Brad and Brian.

Choose Your Person Viewpoint Detailing:

_____
_____
_____
_____
_____
_____
_____
_____
_____
_____
_____
_____
_____
_____
_____
_____
_____
_____
_____
_____
_____
_____
_____
_____
_____
_____
_____
_____
_____

From The Authors

CONGRATULATIONS

You Have Made It Through Writing on the Super Highway!
Next is your final road so…
You've earned a rest! Then get back on the road to your finished
story with

"How To Write Your Book - From an Idea to Your Finished Story"
Book 3 – Crossing the Finish Line

In Book 3

Mechanic-ism's of Writing

Character's SPEAK Up

Your Writing Style

Finishing With Flair

Take Your Story To Market

And Finish with Final Words From Our Authors

So Get Book 3 Now
And Write Your Finished Story!

Golden Quill Press
www.goldenquillpress.com

Words Related to Writing

A

Advance – The amount paid to a writer by a publisher before a book is published. The advance is generally deducted from royalties earned from sales of the finished book.

Agent – A person who represents and acts on behalf of writers.

All rights – The rights contracted to a publisher (magazines, books) to permit the use of a writer's work any time, in any form without paying additional royalties.

Antagonists – A person (characters) who competes with or opposes another. An opponent or adversary.

Assignment – The contract between a writer and editor that confirms dates the writer will complete a project and fees to be paid the writer.

Autobiography – The story of one's own life written or dictated by oneself.

B

Book developer/packager – A business that plans and produces all elements of a book for publishers and producers.

Biography – An account of a person's life written by another.

By-line – The author's name on a published work.

C

Character – A person in a story or play.

Cliché – A trite expression or idea.

Climax – A decisive turning point or action.

Clips – Copies of a writer's work that has been published.

C

Confidant – The person to whom the main character would express undisclosed information the reader needs to know

Conflict – To clash or to be in opposition.

Contemporary – Relating to writing that reflects current trends, themes, and subjects.

Copy – Manuscript pages before being set in type.

Copy editing – The line by line editing of a manuscript.

Copyright – The lawful protection of a writer's work and considered to be in effect at the time of writing or by recording.

Cover letter – A one page, or brief letter to an editor sent with a manuscript.

D

Deadline – The date when a writer's work must be ready.

Denouement – The outcome, solution, or unraveling of a plot.

Description – Technique of describing or picturing by way of words.

Dialogue – The passages of talk or conversations in a play or story.

Disk copy – Circular plate on which data is stored; disk copy of a manuscript.

Draft – First or rough copies of a story, article, or other material.

E

Editing – To revise and make ready a manuscript

Editor – A person who's work is procuring and editing manuscripts

E-mail – Mail sent electronically by a computer.

Epiphany ending – The end of a story that gives the reader a sense of understanding and insight.

Exposition – The writing that explains facts, ideas, who characters are, the setting and related information.

F

Fair use – A provision in copyright law that allows the use of short quotes or passages to be used from copyrighted work.

Fiction – A story or other work of the imagination and portraying imaginary characters and events.

First serial rights – The right to publish materials for the first time before it is in book form.

Flashback – Filling in details in a story to let the reader know something that happened in the past. Also called back story

Flash forward – A device in writing that prepares the reader for events to come without going into specific details. Also called foreshadowing.

Free writing – Unrestrained writing that allows ideas to flow. Also called clustering or brainstorming. Methods of generating fresh ideas.

G

Galleys – The first set of proofs of a manuscript before being prepared in page form.

Genré – A category or type of fiction: Horror, western, romance, science fiction, etc....

H

Hard copy – A copy of a manuscript printed from a computer.

Hook – The lead into a story that keeps the reader interested. To hook or grab interest.

I

Imprint – A publisher's line. Example: Jan, an imprint of Robin House Publishers.

J

Juvenile fiction – stories for children ages 2 to 12.

Justify – Printing in line or flush. As when typing a manuscript, you may not want to justify right margins.

L

Lead-in – The beginning of a new scene.

Lead time – The time between planning a book and the publication date.

Literary agent – The person who represents an author, finds a publisher and negotiates contracts.

M

Mainstream – Fiction that has a prevailing and strong trend.

Manuscript – An author's unpublished work in typewritten pages. Abbreviated ms or mss (plural).

Mass market – Books that appeal to a wide readership and are sold in various outlets such as grocery, stationary and drug stores.

Masthead – A list of a magazine's staff members, their titles and departments.

Metaphor – A figure of speech where a word or phrase used for one thing is applied to another as in imagery. Example: A snowfall of white beard covered the old man's face.

Multiple submissions – Submitting more than one story to the same editor at the same time.

N

Narration – The events in a story related by the person telling the story.

Narrator – The person who tells a story.

O

One-time rights – Permission to reprint an author's work one time only.

Opposition – A person who resists, has an opposite stance or contradicts another.

Outline – A summary of a story or book contents.

P

Pace – The slowing down or speeding up of a story by punctuation, dialogue, or the author's style and use of language.

Pen name – Pseudonym an author chooses to use to conceal his or her own name.

Plot – The events scheme or plan of a story through which characters progress.

Premise – A short explanation of what the story is about.

Proofreading – The careful reading and correcting of errors in a manuscript using proofreader's marks.

Proposal – An offer to write a specific work.

Protagonist – The lead character in a story; the hero.

Public domain – Written material that is no longer copyrighted or has never been copyrighted.

Q

Query letter (a letter of inquiry) – A type of cover letter, usually one page, written to an editor in which the writer proposes a story, book, article, or an idea to the editor.

R

Rejection slip – A note from a publishing house that accompanies the return or refusal of an author's work.

Reprint rights – The right of a publisher to print an article or other work after it has been printed by another publication.

Resolution – The solution to a problem. A decision for future action. The end of a story made clear by an explanation.

Revision – To read carefully and correct, improve, update, or change a manuscript or other writing.

Royalties – A specified percentage paid for the work of an author.

S

SASE – Self addressed stamped envelope sent by an author for the return of work not accepted for publication.

Setting – The time period and location in which a story takes place.

Simultaneous submissions – Sending copies of a manuscript to more than one publisher at the time.

Simile – A figure of speech in which one thing is likened to another. Example: "A river of tears" or "Tears flowed like a river."

Slant – Writing a topic with a different approach.

Slush-pile – The stack of unsolicited manuscripts not likely to be accepted by a publisher.

Subplot – The secondary story running thread-like through the main plot.

Subsidiary rights – All the rights in addition to or other than book rights a published author may agree upon.

Synopsis – A brief summary of a story, usually a page or two, written to interest the editor in the complete work.

T

Tag – The words following the quoted dialogue of a character. Example: "Where are you?" he asked. "I am at the store," she said.

Theme – The central and dominant idea of a story or other work, also called the backbone, the message, or main thread.

Tone – The manner of writing that shows the attitude of the narrator.

Transition – A word, phrase, sentence, or paragraph that relates a preceding topic to a succeeding one. The connecting of one idea to the next.

U

Unsolicited submissions – Manuscripts sent to a publisher without an agency representation or that an editor did not ask to see.

V

Viewpoint – The position from which the narrator tells the story and how the story's action is meant to be seen by the reader.

AUTHORS BIOGRAPHIES

Francine Barish-Stern has been an author for over 40 years, and has received numerous awards for poetry and short stories. Her "Rainbow City" won first place and was published in "The Arts Newspaper." She has been a writer for newspapers and magazines and has worked on over 18 books including, "TELL IT TO THE FUTURE" and "NEW HORIZONS." She has recently finished her first full length novel "Code 47 to B R EV Force." Francine has developed writing programs for all ages and has created and designed materials for numerous businesses. She teaches writing, acting and co-wrote and produced, the play, "The WE Nobody Knows" for Crown Players. Also an accomplished business writer, she has specialized in seminars on telemarketing. Francine has recently added photography to her creative interests and has won major awards for her exhibits. Recently, her photograph, "Falls at the Bridge" was exhibited at the Art Museum of Western Virginia. All her art work are produced exclusively as Art on Gold and can be seen at Creations in Roanoke Virginia. .

Bobbi R. Madry, Educational Director for The Write Source and Golden Quill Press also serves as consultant, author and editor. During her career which has spanned more than 50 years, she has also served as senior editor of numerous books and educational publications for major New York City publishers. She has also written book reviews for national magazines. Bobbi served as Associate Publisher for a New York newspaper where she also mentored aspiring writers. She has received numerous awards for writing and community service. Bobbi teaches writing and poetry and holds degrees in the Arts and Behavioral Sciences. Her published works: Human Relations For Business - A Vocational Dictionary - The Job Seeker's Guide - Love Makes The Difference - Work Force 2000 (co-author) - The Professional Models Handbook (co-author). She has been the co-author and editor for Tell it to the Future and New Horizons as well editor of over 18 books published by Golden Quill Press, and is presently authoring several new books.

Books By Golden Quill Press

CODE 47 to BREV Force
By: F.Barish-Stern

The adventures of The BREV Force: College Students fighting to defeat the evils of Controller, a renegade computer virus, threatening to take over the world

TELL IT TO THE FUTURE
BY: Francine R. Cefola (F.Barish-Stern)   & Bobbi R. Madry

TELL IT TO THE FUTURE-Have I Got A Story For You ... about the Twentieth Century leaves personal messages with timelines and stories about our hopes, dreams, or events that impacted on, or changed our lives. Each story focuses on events from a specific decade of the twentieth century with descriptions that reflect the color of the times. Some are witty, some filled with wisdom, while others pull at your heart strings.

LOVE MAKES A DIFFERENCE -
BY: Mary Bianchini and Bobbi Madry

Arriving as an immigrant with her mother in the early 1900's, Mary grew up to become one of the most influential figures in Rockland County, N.Y. Honored by four Presidents and in the Congressional Record, Mary shares her advice about family, community service and reaching her dreams.

NEW HORIZONS -
Life's Poetic Connections
BY: Francine R. Cefola (F. Barish-Stern)
& Bobbi R. Madry

Poetry is the art that speaks to our hearts and minds. Like a beautiful painting or a musical composition, this collection of poetry will take you into worlds limited only by your imagination... from the splendor of a sunset to tasting candy, to memories from a rocking chair ... **Let These Poems Take You To Your Own New Horizons!!**

CHALLENGING MESSAGES
FROM BEYOND

BY: Marjorie Struck

Does the Spiritual World have a message for us? Can we learn to understand that communication? Marjorie Struck certainly believes . This is her personal story of how a message form Beyond changed her life. Informative, at times shocking, but ultimately a journey that reveals a side of the spiritual world that can transform you-forever. Marjorie invites you along to witness how this revelation helped her understand the connection between life and beyond- and how souls in the after life help us to find the Light!

COMPASSION'S LURE

BY: Kathleen Lukens

This is the story of a visionary. Kathy Lukens founder of Camp Venture - advocate for all people with special needs stood up for the rights and deeds of those who could not fight for themselves. With words backed by tireless efforts, Kathy made the impossible happen for the developmentally disabled- a home and the proper attention to their needs. She was truly one of the Great Women of our times.

the GRANPA SPIDER stories

BY: Granpa Spider

A delightful story for children of all ages. Granpa Spider weaves a web of adventure and intrigue, mystery and fun! Along with his Arachnid friends, Penelope, The Colonel ,   and others we journey into the exciting world of the web. As Shamrock McGee says, "May the wind be at your web. May your web be in the trees. May cicada be chattering. May there be a host of bees, And, may the web that you spin be serving all your needs... "

MAE SINGS
ABOUT SHORT VOWELS

BY: Karen A. Coleman

"Mae Sings About Short Vowels," was developed by Karen Coleman, as a method for teaching music, while learning vowel sounds. The book uses songs and a vowel recognition technique in an interactive way to help students improve reading skills while learning musical notes

OPENING THE DOOR
TO A BRIGHTER FUTURE

BY: Daniel Windheim

After writing and publishing," It's Not All Black And White" which dealt with the experiences of my son, Dan ,sustaining a traumatic brain injury and the efforts he made to recover and build a productive life, we decided that many of the lessons both Dan and I learned from that experience might have relevance to others recovering from injuries or illnesses. We therefore set out to write a book detailing ten key strategies that could help individuals in their recovery efforts and to share the experiences of some survivors as they struggle to return to a healthy life. As Dan notes'" There is not time to waste focusing on the negative, but we need to take what we have and make the most out of things."

THE POEM BOOK

BY: Daniel Windheim

A brain injury victim of a car accident young Daniel Windheim's life is turned upside down. He turns to poetry to express his frustration, anger and and to take the reader on a beautiful journey through recuperation and new life challenges. Daniel Windheim is truly a shining hero, overcoming life's worst experience. "I remain practical; but a realist, and accept what I am. Life is good, and there is goodness in life."

SWEET MERCY

BY: Rebecca H. Cofer

Katherine Ryder peels away the decades of family secrets to tell her story of growing up in Fairburn, Georgia at the turn of the century - 1900. She battles many obstacles to free herself from small town life and her autocratic mother and moves to Atlanta. In the big city she is betrayed by the man she loves. But her generous heart and hard work pay off, bringing her joy and fulfillment in the end.

THERE IS HOPE

BY: Debby Paine

There Is Hope is a collection of religious poetry about the struggles, pains questions and fears we all face. Debby's love of family, church and community is portrayed as she searches for and reaches toward God to find hope. These poems from the heart-for the heart, will reach out to everyone searching for hope. " Reach for it. Hold on to it. 'Hope is There.' "

Other books marketed by Golden Quill Press:

YOU ARE WHAT YOU WEAR

BY:William Thourlby

"First impressions" are lasting. YOU ARE WHAT YOU WEAR will help you make the right "first impression." Develop skills that are cost effective because they not only increase the quality of life in the workplace, contribute to employee morale and embellish the company image, they play a major role in developing a person's self image and generating profits. The lack of these skills can be highly visible and costly for any person or company in every day and age.

PASSPORT TO POWER

BY: William Thourlby

Part practical, part primer, part visionary, Passport to Power, gives the reader background and formulas to follow to acquire and master international communication skills and provide the keys to unlocking human potential for success as a leader in the new global village of today.

TELL IT TO THE FUTURE

Have I got A Story For You…
About the Twentieth Century

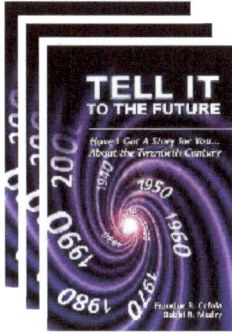

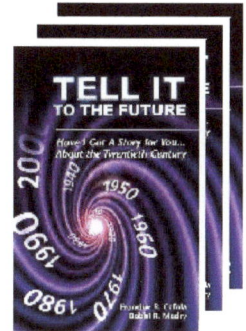

Stories to make

You laugh, Stories to make

You cry

Stories to bring

Back memories of a Time Gone By

Stories of a time that

Most of us never knew

Coming to America…

Going off to war

Just to name a few

These stories vividly paint a portrait of America during the decades

Of the 20th Century…

Am America you'll never forget

GREAT REFERENCE and RESOURCE Book
For the Twentieth Century

BE SURE YOU

TELL IT TO THE FUTURE

Order at www.goldenquillpress.com

www.ingramcontent.com/pod-product-compliance
Lightning Source LLC
LaVergne TN
LVHW072052070426
835508LV00002B/55